# POEMS OF
# ARAB ANDALUSIA

## Translated by Cola Franzen
from the Spanish versions of Emilio García Gómez

## CITY LIGHTS BOOKS
San Francisco

Cover image: Fragment of a poem by Ibn Zamrak from the
Alhambra, the Royal Palace, in Granada, Spain.
Book design: Patricia Fujii


Library of Congress Cataloging-in-Publication Data
Poems of Arab Andalusia / translated by Cola Franzen.
          p. cm.
      ISBN 0-87286-242-9
          1. Arabic poetry — Spain — Andalusia — Translation into
English.
2. Arabic poetry — 750-1258 — Translation into English. 3.
English poetry — Translations from Arabic.    I. Franzen, Cola.
PJ8414.P6    1989
892'.713408094680— dc20                                      89-15815
                                                                  CIP

**Visit our website: www.citylights.com**

CITY LIGHTS BOOKS are edited by Lawrence Ferlinghetti and
Nancy J. Peters and published at the City Lights Bookstore, 261
Columbus Avenue, San Francisco, CA 94133.

# CONTENTS

Note: The titles in Spanish and page numbers in brackets refer to the poems in
*Poemas Arábigoandaluces*, by Emilio García Gómez, Colección Austral, Espasa-
Calpe, S.A., Madrid, fifth edition, 1971.

# ACKNOWLEDGEMENTS

My heartfelt thanks and gratitude go first to Claudio Guillén, who was an active participant in this project from the very beginning, who encouraged and helped me in many practical ways, including checking the final translations; to Don Wellman, whose interest, keen critical reading, suggestions, and insistence on striving for excellence contributed in major ways to the book; to the members of my poetry workshop who read the early versions of these poems and whose comments and insights were invaluable; to Nancy Peters at City Lights who with her warmth and expertise made the transition from typescript to published book smooth and pleasurable. I wish to express special thanks to James T. Monroe, so generous and knowledgable, to whom I am indebted for the correct transliteration of the names of the poets and Arabic words, as well as for other helpful suggestions; to Emilio García Gómez, my deep appreciation and admiration and my thanks for his generosity in granting me permission to translate the *Poemas*; and finally to my husband, Wolfgang Franzen, whose enthusiasm for this project never lessened and whose timely nudges kept it burning bright even during fallow periods, my thanks and my love: to him I dedicate this book.

# TRANSLATOR'S NOTE

Browsing in a bookstore a number of years ago I came across a little paperback book called *Poemas Arábigoandaluces*, an anthology of poems from Moorish Spain of the tenth through the thirteenth centuries, collected and translated into contemporary Spanish by Emilio García Gómez. I immediately fell in love with the book and began to translate some of the poems into English, simply to be able to show friends who couldn't read Spanish some hint of the treasure I had found. Even those first attempts aroused considerable interest, because the poems were very little known in this country. Centuries of marvelous poetry had been lying submerged, lost from sight for the general reader. So I was encouraged and helped to continue. Since I do not read Arabic, I based my versions on García Gómez's prose translations. My aim was to try to re-create a poem in English that would find an echo in today's poetical sensibility, reverberate in the modern soul.

I made my selection from the fifth edition of the *Poemas* (Colección Austral, Espasa-Calpe, Madrid, 1971). James T. Monroe, professor of Arabic and Comparative Literature at the University of California, Berkeley, has very kindly supplied me with the correct transliterations into English of proper names and Arabic words to conform with modern usage. Dates of births and deaths, or reigns, in the case of kings, were taken from the *Poemas*; a few corrections have been made by Professor Monroe in light of more recent research. I have arranged the poems in chronological order, without the traditional breakdown into geographical subdivisions common for Arab anthologists and followed by García Gómez in his arrangement of the *Poemas*.

# INTRODUCTION
*Cola Franzen*

*Poemas Arábigoandaluces* is based on an earlier anthology, the codex of Ibn Sa'īd dated 1243, which the great Spanish Arabist, Emilio García Gómez, acquired in Cairo in 1928, then unedited, unpublished, and completed unknown. It was called *Rāyāt al-Mubarrizīn wa-ghāyāt al-mumayyizīn* (The Banners of the Champions and the Standards of the Select Ones). García Gómez says that while he was working on a complete translation of the codex, a scholarly treatise,[1] he included some of the poems in an article published in the *Revista del Occidente* in August of 1928. Those and others added later make up the *Poemas*. In his prologue, García Gómez's only claim for his translations was that that they "allow us to see, even if from afar, what Arab-Andalusian poetry was like in the tenth, eleventh, twelfth and thirteenth centuries. Enough, however, if the ancient saying is true, that a few verses can reveal the soul of a people better than long pages of history." As we shall see, García Gómez was far too modest, for his *"librito,"* his little book, as he liked to call it, changed the landscape of Spanish poetry.

Writing ten years after the first edition of the *Poemas* appeared, he said: "When the first edition of this little book came out in 1930, I was not prepared for the warm reception it received from critics and readers. This new taste of the soul of our divine Andalusia was a surprise, no doubt." He went on to say that the scholars, artists and poets of the time — the poets who became the Generation of 27 — had turned their attention to metaphor and image. "My collection based on Ibn Sa'īd's codex, which is precisely a collection of metaphorical fragments, was of double interest to our poetical circles for being at one and the same time very old and very new."

His little book has been in print ever since and continues to inspire and enchant Spanish language readers and poets alike. Rafael Alberti was one of those poets of the Generation of 27 who saw the poems when they first appeared. Speaking of the occasion in an interview with Natalia Calamai some years ago,[2] he said: "The book of Arab-Andalusian poetry of Emilio García Gómez that appeared between 1928 and 1929[3] was a revelation for me and had a great influence on my work, but above all influenced the work of Federico García Lorca. Federico wrote a book of qaṣīdas, *El Diván del Tamarit*, and other similar poems that would not have been possible if it were not for García Gómez's book. I was very impressed by that poetry, which up to then had been poorly known from 19th-century translations, and suddenly it appeared, due to the work of a rigorous scholar of the first rank, with a new sense of what translation should be, of what poetry is, a man after all of our own Generation of 27, a profoundly poetical generation. That book opened our eyes to all that Andalusian past, and brought it so close to us that it left me with a great preoccupation for those writers, those Andalusian writers, Arabs and Jews, born in Spain . . . . Those superb writers link up perfectly with our poets of the Golden Age. If one studies Arab-Andalusian poetry carefully, so full of metaphors and miniaturism, we will see that there is a continuity with the later poetry, of Góngora, Soto de Rojas, and centuries later, with our own."

About Lorca's *Diván*, García Gómez recalls that in September 1934, he and Lorca were having dinner with a group of friends in Granada. " . . . we were talking, talking — and behind our image of Granada there kept appearing — like those geometrical figures where hidden edges are indicated with dotted lines — the idea of another earlier Granada, purified in the hypothesis, where other people sang in another language to the sound of other guitars.

"Exchanging news of literary projects, I said to Lorca that I was planning to dedicate a book to an illustrious Arab — Ibn Zamrak — whose poems had been published in the most luxurious edition that the world has ever known — on the walls and around the fountain rims of the Alhambra itself. Lorca then told us that he had written a collection of qaṣīdas and ghazals, that is, a *Dīwān*, in homage to those ancient poets of Granada, and he would call it *El Diván del Tamarit*, Tamarit being the name of an orchard belonging to his family where many of the poems had been written.

"Antonio Gallego Burín, Dean of the Faculty of Letters of the University of Granada, asked him for the manuscript. Lorca agreed with pleasure. Francisco Prieto offered to design the cover. I promised to write these lines. . . ."

The project went very slowly and before the book could be published, Lorca was assassinated in Granada by Falangist troops on August 19, 1936, in the early days of the Civil War. ("And the crime took place in Granada," Antonio Machado was to write later, "imagine — poor Granada! in his Granada. . . .")[4] Lorca's *Diván* had to wait 47 years to be published in Spain. It finally appeared in 1981 with García Gómez's original prologue, some of which is quoted above.[5] Earlier editions were brought out in 1940 in New York and Buenos Aires.[6]

Most critics who have looked carefully at the *Diván* agree that Lorca did not attempt to copy the Arab-Andalusian poets, but to immerse himself in their poetry in order to reveal the soul, the essence, and recast it in his own manner. But he did explore how close he could come in Spanish to some formal aspects of classical Arabic poetry. Two of the poems are in monorhyme, traditional in classical Arabic prosody: *Ghazal no. VII* has 12 couplets all ending in *o* and the *qasīda VIII* uses *a* as the final vowel throughout. There is also a great deal of internal rhyming in *a*, making this perhaps the most beautiful poem in the book. ["La muchacha dorada / se bañaba en el agua / y el agua se doraba."] Lorca also used many of the same themes and often strikingly similar imagery. Ibn Jākh in "Leavetaking" says: ". . . tears crept like scorpions / over the fragrant roses / of their cheeks." Here is Lorca, in *ghazal no. III*, "Del amor desesperado": "But I will go / even though a scorpion sun gnaws my cheek."

It is fun to find such similarities but the fact is that the Arab-Andalusian poetry works more like one of those fanciful streams designed for the Generalife that run underground, then pop up when least expected right under one's feet. The Arab-Andalusian poetry was a missing tile of the rich cultural mosaic of Spain. When it was slipped into place, a gap was filled. A part of our cultural past as well as theirs had been lost and has now been recovered. What can often be found in contemporary poetry in Spanish is something like a whiff, a fragrance, sometimes a friendly nod of recognition on the part of a poet of today to those "who sang in another language to the sound of other guitars." Here is Jorge Luis Borges in "Poema Conjetural": "Pisan mis pies la sombra de las lanzas / que me buscan. . ." ["I step on the shadow of the lances / that come in search of me. . ."]

The appeal and enduring beauty of these poems whose glow still reaches us even after being dismantled and refashioned in other languages cannot be explained but merely marveled at. Ibn Sa'īd, who was poet as well as historian, geographer, bellelettrist, and compiler of the anthology, said he wished to include only those few fragments "whose idea is more subtle than the West Wind, and whose language is more beautiful than a pretty face." And García Gómez tells us that indeed except for some complete *dīwāns* and a few celebrated *qaṣīdas*, the large part of Arab-Andalusian poetry has come down to us "in fragments, shattered, although in iridescent diamond dust."

Who were the fabricators of those verbal jewels? There were kings (Al-Mu'tamid;), viziers (Ibn 'Ammār of Silves), princes, (Marwān ibn 'Abd al-Raḥmān), califs, qāḍīs, rulers of all sorts ('Abd al-Raḥmān V al-Mustaẓhir, Ibn 'Iyāḍ, 'Umar ibn 'Umar), doctors (Abū l-Ḥajjāj ibn 'Utba, Abū l-Ṣalt Umayyah), Ibn Sa'īd al-Maghribī himself, and others known simply as poets, some great ones, like Ibn Zaydūn and Ibn Ḥazm, both of Córdoba. After going through a lengthy list, García Gómez concludes: "They were all poets!" It was said that in Silves, part of the kingdom of Sevilla, any laborer driving his ox cart would be capable of improvising a poem on any theme suggested to him. High officials — kings, viziers, ambassadors — wrote their invitations, excuses, insults, autobiographies in poetry. "All poetry!" García Gómez says, "A lot of it artificial and false, but still from time to time blossoms appeared

iv

bearing the most noble and eternal human sentiments."

And so after our various meanders we come back to the poems written in, for, and about the place they called al-Andaluz, the garden. Seldom has so much love been lavished on a land. Like a man wooing a woman, the Arabs courted, cossetted, adored and adorned Spain with orchards, gardens, fountains and pools, cities and palaces, and century after century sang her praises in unforgettable verse. The pleasures and sorrows of their days. Love, friendship, revelry. The flora and fauna. The beautiful women. Horses and war. And the water. Oh, the water. The courtship lasted almost 800 years; the suitor was rejected in the end, and we are left with the love letters.

FOOTNOTES

1. *El libro de las banderas de los campiones*, edited, annotated, and translated into Spanish. Published in Madrid in 1942 by the Instituto de Valencia de Don Juan.
2. R. Alberti: *Prosas*, Alianza Editorial, Madrid, 1980.
3. Some of the poems, as noted earlier, were published in the *Revista del Occidente* in 1928; the book first appeared in 1930.
4. From the poem, "El crimen fue en Granada."
5. Alianza Editorial, Madrid, edited, with an introduction and notes by Mario Hernández.
6. Revista Hispánica Moderna, of the Hispanic Institute, New York, and Instituto de filología, Buenos Aires.

READING

My eye frees what the page imprisons:
the white the white and the black the black.

> *Ibn 'Ammār*
> *(d. 1086) (Silves)*

# WHITE SKIN

I have never seen
nor heard of such a thing

her modesty turns
pearl into carnelian.

Her face is so clear
that when you gaze
on its perfections

you see your own face
reflected.

Ibn 'Abd Rabbihi
*(860-940) (Córdoba)*

# MY BELOVED COMES

You came to me just before
the Christians rang their bells.
The half-moon was rising
looking like an old man's eyebrow
or a delicate instep.

And although it was still night,
when you came, a rainbow
gleamed on the horizon,
showing as many colors
as a peacock's tail.

Ibn Ḥazm
*(994-1063) (Córdoba)*

# CHASTITY

Although she was ready to give
herself to me, I abstained
and did not accept
the temptation Satan offered.

She came unveiled in the night.
Illuminated by her face,
night put aside its shadowy
veils as well.

Each one of her glances
could cause hearts to turn over.

But I clung to the divine precept
that condemns lust and reined in
the capricious horses of my passion
so that my instinct
would not rebel against chastity.

And so I passed the night with her
like a thirsty little camel
whose muzzle keeps it from nursing.

She was a field of fruit and flowers
offering one like me no other enjoyment
than sight and scent.

Know then that I am not
one of those beasts gone wild
who take gardens for pastures.

Ibn Faraj
*(10th century) (Jaén)*

# GRAINFIELD

Look at the ripe wheat
bending before the wind

like squadrons of horsemen
fleeing in defeat, bleeding
from the wounds of the poppies.

Ibn 'Iyāḍ
*(1083-1149) (Central Andalusia)*

# REFLECTION OF WINE

Light passing through wine
reflects on the fingers
of the cupbearer
dyeing them red
as juniper stains
the muzzle of the antelope.

**Abū l-Ḥasan ʿAlī ibn Ḥiṣn**
*(11th century) (Sevilla)*

# SERENE EVENING

A serene evening.
We spend it drinking wine.


The sun, going down,
lays its cheek against the earth
to rest.


The breeze lifts
the coattails of the hills.
The skin of the sky
is as smooth as the pelt
of the river.


How lucky we are to find
this spot for our sojourn
with doves cooing
for our greater delight.

Birds sing,
branches sigh
and darkness drinks up
the red wine of sunset.

Muḥammad ibn Ghālib al-Ruṣāfī
*(d. 1177) (Ruzafa, Valencia)*

# BLUE RIVER

The river of diaphanous waters
murmuring between its banks
would have you believe
it is a stream of pearls.

At midday tall trees
cover it with shadows
turning it the color of metal.

So now you see it, blue,
wrapped in brocade,
like a warrior in armor
resting in the shade of his banner.

Muḥammad ibn Ghālib al-Ruṣāfī

# THE BEAUTY AT THE REVELS

Like a young tree in springtime
her slim waist sways
over the sand dunes of her hips.
From her branches my heart
garners fruits of fire.


The blond hair falling over
her temples draws a *lām*
on the page of her cheek,
silver flowed over gold.


The glass of red nectar
between her white fingers
is the day being born
of the dawn.


The wine is the rising sun,
her mouth the setting sun,
the hand of the assiduous
cupbearer, the east.

The wine-sun setting
in the delicious west
of her lips
brings dawn to her cheeks.

The Umayyad Prince Marwān ibn ʿAbd al-Raḥmān
*(d. 1009) (Central Andalusia)*

---

*lām* — the 23rd letter of the Arabic alphabet (  ﻝ  ).

# THE ROOSTER

Sparks shooting from his eyes
and wearing a poppy on his head
he arises to announce the death of night.


When he crows he himself listens
to his call to prayer
then hurriedly beats his great wings
against his body.


It seems the king of Persia
gave him his crown
and Maria the Copt, sister of Moses,
hung the pendant around his neck.


He snitched the peacock's dressiest coat
and to top it off
his strutting walk
he stole from a duck.

Al-As'ad Ibrāhīm ibn Billīṭah
*(11th century) (Toledo)*

# THE GOBLETS

The goblets were heavy
when they were brought to us

but filled with fine wine
they became so light

they were on the point of flying away
with all their contents

just as our bodies are lightened
by the spirits.

Idrīs ibn al-Yamānī
*(11th century) (Ibiza)*

13

# SATIRE

Although you present perfect
musical soirées to entertain us
let's get this straight:

the singers are flies,
the flute players mosquitos
and the dancers fleas.

Ibn Sharaf
*(d. 1068) (Qayrawān)*

# THE EMBROIDERED WRAP

Her glance, like a gazelle's,
her throat, that of a white deer,
lips red as wine,
teeth white as sea foam.

Tipsiness made her languid.
The gold-embroidered figures
of her wrap swirled round her,
brilliant stars around the moon.

During the night love's hands
wrapped us in a garment of embraces
ripped open
by the hands of dawn.

Ibn Khafāja
*(1058-1138) (Alcira)*

# LEAVETAKING

On the morning they left
we said goodbye
filled with sadness
for the absence to come.

Inside the palanquins
on the camels' backs
I saw their faces beautiful as moons
behind veils of gold cloth.

Beneath the veils
tears crept like scorpions
over the fragrant roses
of their cheeks.

These scorpions do not harm
the cheek they mark.
They save their sting
for the heart of the sorrowful lover.

Ibn Jākh
*(11th century) (Badajoz)*

# SPLIT MY HEART

How I wish I could split my heart
with a knife
put you inside
then close up my chest

so that you would be in my heart
and not in another's
until the resurrection
and the day of judgment.

There you would stay while I lived
and after my death
you would remain buried deep in my heart
in the darkness of the tomb.

Ibn Ḥazm
*(994-1063) (Córdoba)*

# WALNUT

Its covering is composed
of two halves so joined
it's a pleasure to see:
like eyelids closed in sleep.

Cleave it with a knife
and you will say the convex side
is an eye bulging out
straining to see

while the inside is an ear
because of the convolutions
and crevices.

**Abū Bakr Muḥammad ibn al-Qūṭiyyah**
*(11th century) (Sevilla)*

19

# THE STORK

She is an immigrant from other lands.
When she stretches out her ebony wings
shows her ivory body
opens her sandalwood beak
and laughs with great guffaws
it's a sign of good weather.

Ghālib ibn Ribāḥ al-Ḥajjām
*(11th century) (Toledo)*

# AFTER THE REVELS

When the wine he drank
put him to sleep and the eyes
of the watchmen closed also

I approached him timidly
like one who seeks to come close,
but on the sly, pretending not to.

I crept toward him imperceptible
as a dream, moved myself close
to him, softly as a breath.

I kissed his throat, a white jewel,
drank the vivid red of his mouth

and so passed my night with him
deliciously, until darkness smiled,
showing the white teeth of dawn.

## Ibn Shuhayd
*(992-1034) (Córdoba)*

# BUBBLES

I say to the cupbearer:

Give me your best,
change my silver
for the gold of wine.
In it I'll drown my sorrows.

On the surface foamy bubbles
form a pattern of white fingers
like those of an inveterate drinker
always holding a bottle in his hand.

'Ubādah ibn Mā' al-Samā'
*(d. 1030) (area of Córdoba)*

23

# THE WHITE STALLION

Pale as the morning star
in the hour of sunrise

he advances proudly,
caparisoned with a saddle of gold.

One who saw him going with me
into battle, envied me and said:

"Who bridled Dawn with the Pleiades?
 Who saddled lightning with the half moon?"

Abū l-Ṣalt Umayyah
*(1067-1134) (Denia)*

# SLAVE BOY

They shaved his head
to clothe him in ugliness
out of jealousy and fear
of his beauty.

They erased the night
and left him in dawn.

Yūsuf ibn Hārūn al-Ramādī
*(d. 1022) (Córdoba)*

# SUMMER STORM

The sky darkens:
flowers open their mouths
and search for the udders
of the nurturing rain

as battalions of black
water-laden clouds
parade majestically past
flashing their golden swords.

Ibn Shuhayd
*(992-1034) (Córdoba)*

# MOURNING IN ANDALUSIA

If white is the color
of mourning in Andalusia,
it is a proper custom.

Look at me,
I dress myself in the white
of white hair
in mourning for youth.

Abū l-Ḥasan al-Ḥuṣrī
*("The Blind Man"), (d. 1095) (Eastern Andalusia)*

# REPROACH

My nights are much longer
since you insisted on banishing me
from your side,

oh, gazelle who delays
her promise and does not keep
the word she gave!

Have you forgotten
the night we spent
on a bed of roses

when stars on the horizon
gleamed like pearls
against lapis lazuli.

'Abd al-Raḥmān V al-Mustaẓhir
*(d. 1024) (Córdoba)*

# LILIES

The hands of spring
have built crenellated castles
atop the lily stalks:

silver parapets
where knights defend the prince
with golden swords.

Ibn Darrāj al-Qasṭallī
*(958-1030) (Córdoba)*

# ABSENCE

Every night I scan
the heavens with my eyes
seeking the star
that you are contemplating.

I question travellers
from the four corners of the earth
hoping to meet one
who has breathed your fragrance.

When the wind blows
I make sure it blows in my face:
the breeze might bring me
news of you.

I wander over roads
without aim, without purpose.
Perhaps a song
will sound your name.


Secretly I study
every face I see
hoping against hope
to glimpse a trace of your beauty.

Abū Bakr al-Ṭurṭūshī
*(1059-1126) (Eastern Andalusia)*

# FRAGMENTS FROM THE "QAṢĪDA IN THE RHYME OF NŪN"

Now we are far apart
one from the other
my heart has dried up
but my tears keep falling.


In losing you my days
have turned black.
When I was with you
even my nights were white.


It's as though we never spent
that night together
with no third presence
save our two selves made one,


a night our lucky star
caused even gossips
who would spy on us
to turn away their eyes.

We were two secrets
held by the heart of darkness
until the tongue of dawn
threatened to denounce us.

Ibn Zaydūn
*(1003-1070) (Córdoba)*

---

*nūn* — 25th letter of the Arabic alphabet ( ن ).

# WRITTEN FROM AL-ZAHRĀ'*

From al-Zahrā'
I remember you with passion.
The horizon is clear,
the earth's face serene.


The breeze grows faint
with the coming of dawn.
It seems to pity me
and lingers, full of tenderness.


The meandering waterway
with its silvery waters
shows a sparkling smile.
It resembles a necklace
unclasped and thrown aside.


A day like those delicious ones
now gone by
when seizing the dream of destiny
we were thieves of pleasure.

---

*al-Zahrā', referring to Madīnat al-Zahrā', the palace complex outside
Córdoba. (The ruins are still extant.) The gardens are said to have been
more splendid and extensive than the Generalife in Granada.

Today, alone,
I distract myself with flowers
that attract my eyes like magnets.
The wind roughhouses with them
bending them over.


The blossoms are eyes.
They see my sleeplessness
and weep for me;
their iridescent tears overflow
staining the calyx.


In the bright sun
red buds light up the rose bushes
making the morning
brighter still.


Fragrant breaths come from the pome
of the waterlilies,
sleepyheads with eyes
half-opened by dawn.

Everything stirs up the memory
of my passion for you
still intact in my chest
although my chest might seem
too narrow to contain it.

If, as I so desire,
we two could again be made one,
that day would be the noblest
of all days.

Would God grant calm to my heart
if it could cease to remember you
and refrain from flying
to your side
on wings trembling with desire?

If this passing breeze
would consent to carry me along,
it would put down at your feet
a man worn out by grief.

Oh, my most precious jewel,
the most sublime,
the one preferred by my soul,
as if lovers dealt in jewels!

In times gone by
we demanded of each other
payments of pure love
and were happy as colts
running free in a pasture.

But now I am the only one
who can boast of being loyal.
You left me
and I stay here,
still sad, still loving you.

Ibn Zaydūn

# INSOMNIA

When the bird of sleep
thought to nest
in my eye

it saw the eyelashes
and flew away
for fear of nets.

Abū 'Amir ibn al-Ḥammārah
*(12th century) (Eastern Andalusia)*

# IN THE BATTLE

I remembered Sulayma
when the ardor of the battle
was like that of my body
when I left her.

I saw her slim waist
among the lances
and when they leaned toward me
I embraced them.

Abū l-Ḥasan ibn al-Qabṭurnuh
*(12th century) (Badajoz)*

# POOL WITH TURTLES

This beautiful pool,
a brimming eye,
has thick eyelashes of flowers.


Turtles cavort
in their capes of green algae.


Now they squabble on the bank
but when winter comes
they'll dive below and hide.


At play they resemble
Christian soldiers
wearing on their backs
their leather shields.

Ibn Sārah
*(d. 1123) (Santarem)*

# THE BRAZIER

With the cold stinging
like scorpions tonight
the brazier is our remedy.

Its glow cuts warm covers
out of the dark; beneath them
the cold can't find us.

We sit around the vessel of fire
as though it were a bowl of wine
from which we are all drinking.

Sometimes it allows us to come near it
and other times it pushes us back,
as a mother sometimes gives the breast
and other times takes it away.

Ibn Sārah

# RAIN OVER THE RIVER

The wind does the delicate work
of a goldsmith
crimping water into mesh
for a coat of mail.

Then comes the rain
and rivets the pieces together
with little nails.

Abū l-Qāsim al-Manīshī (called 'Aṣā l-A'mā)
*(12th century) (Sevilla)*

# APOLOGY

Don't cross me off as fickle
because a singing voice
has captured my heart.

One must be serious sometimes
and lighthearted at other times:

like wood from which come
both the singer's lute
and the warrior's bow.

Ibrāhīm ibn 'Uthmān
*(12th century) (Córdoba)*

# HONEY RIVER

Stop beside Honey River
stop and ask

about a night I stayed there
until dawn, despite the gossips,

drinking the wine that comes
from the mouth or cutting
the rose of bashfulness.

We embraced like the limbs
of the trees embrace
over the stream.

There were cups of cool wine;
the Northwind was our cupbearer.

Flowers offered us
the aloe's fragrance.

Reflections of floating lights
pointed like lances
at the cuirasse of the river.

There we stayed until
the jewels of frost
forced us to separate.

The nightingale's song
made me feel sadder still.

Ibn Abī Rawḥ
*(12th century) (Algeciras)*

# PETITION FOR A FALCON

Oh, king,
whose fathers were eagles
and of the most exalted rank!

You, who have encircled my neck
with favors precious as pearls
and strung like pearls on a string:
Adorn, now, my hand with a falcon.

Honor me with one with clean wings
and plumage shaped by the north wind.

How proud I will be
to go out with him into the dawn
and with my hand outwit the wind
to take the free with the fettered.

'Abd al-'Azīz ibn al-Qabṭurnuh
*(d. after 1126) (Badajoz)*

# INVITATION

A morning damp with dew
and the earth's cheek
covered with green stubble.
Your friend invites you

to enjoy two simmering pots
already giving off
a savory odor,
some perfumes,
a carafe of wine,
a delicious place,

and I could offer more
if I wanted to;
but it's not seemly
to entertain friends
with too much pomp.

'Abd al-'Azīz ibn al-Qabṭurnuh

# TIDE IN THE GUADALQUIVIR

When the West Wind ripped the river's tunic
the river overflowed its banks
to pursue and take revenge;

but the doves laughed, and made fun
from a sheltering thicket,
and the river, shame-faced,
crawled back into his bed
to hide under its veil.

Ibn Safr al-Marīnī
*(12th century) (Almería)*

# THE VALLEY OF ALMERÍA

Valley of Almería!
God grant that I never see
myself deprived of you!
When I look on you I tremble
as an Indian sword trembles
at the moment of tempering.

And you, friend, here beside me,
enjoy this time, for there are delights
in this paradise not to be found
in the eternal one.

See how excited the river is?
Listen to its murmured applause
sounding beneath the dancing trees
that arch over it
wearing garlands of blossoms.

The branches sweep their sleeves
over the silvered surface of the river
then lift them up
scattering pearls.

Wind crimps the water into ridges
giving it the look of a steel file,
then covers it with scales
like silver-plated armor
or the skin of a cutlass fish.

Ibn Safr al-Marīnī

# NIGHT OF LOVE

When the sun bowed low
before leaving us
I made her promise to visit me
like another sun
the moment the moon
started its nocturnal voyage.


And she came like bright dawn
opening a path through the night
or like the wind
skimming the surface of the river.


The horizon all around me
breathed out perfume
announcing her arrival
as the fragrance precedes a flower.


I went over the traces
of her steps with my kisses
as the reader goes over
the letters of a line.

While night slept,
love was kept awake
by her reed-waist, dune-hips
and face beautiful as the moon.


Part of the night I spent
embracing her
and part kissing her
until the banner of dawn
summoned us to leave
and our circle of embraces was broken.


Oh, fateful night!
Hold back the hour of sundering!

Ibn Safr al-Marīnī

# DRINKING POEM

When I saw the day
going off dying
and night approach
full of youth

when the sun was sprinkling
the last saffron rays
over the hills

and beginning to sift shadows
of black musk powder
over the valleys

then I caused the moon of wine
to come out.
You were the planet Mercury
and our guests, accompanying stars.

Ibn Sirāj
*(d. 1114) (Córdoba)*

# SCENE OF LOVE

When night came trailing shadows
I gave her wine to drink
dark and fragrant as musk powder.

I gripped her as tightly
as a warrior his sword.
Her braids were the scabbards
that hung from my shoulders.

When the sweet weight of sleep
overpowered her
I loosened her embrace
and moved her from my chest

to save her from sleeping
on a palpitating pillow!

**Ibn Baqī**
*(d. 1145) (Córdoba)*

# FIESTA IN A GARDEN

In the morning dark
feelings of desire
whirled round us, spheres
of dalliance and pleasure.


We were in a garden.
A cloud armed with a steely
sword of lightning
poured out the morning's drink.


Red wine, then mounds of myrtle
for our pillows.
We looked like kings
on our green thrones.


Love was stringing beads
for our merrymaking.
We were the pearls,
endearing words the strands.

Young women with lance-like breasts
attacked us, provoking us to war.
To defend ourselves
we wore no other armor
than our capes of fur.

Delicious faces were
uncovered for us:
white moons
amid the night of black braids.

Abū l-Qāsim ibn al-Saqqāṭ
*(12th century) (Málaga)*

# THE PROCURESS

She enjoys her bad reputation.
For someone out at night
she provides better cover
than the night itself.

She enters every house
and nobody knows
just how far she goes.

She's always courteous and friendly
to everyone she meets;
her steps never bother the neighbors.

Her cape is never folded;
it's busier than a flag
in the midst of battle.

When she learned
how useful she is
she also learned the difference
between crime and cleverness.

She may not know
where the mosque is
but she knows the location
of all the taverns.

She's always smiling,
seems very pious,
knows lots of jokes and stories

is good at mathematics
and can cast horoscopes
and spells.

She can't buy a pair of shoes
with what is in her purse
but in the midst of misery
she is rich.

She is such a smooth talker
she could probably
mix fire and water.

## Abū Ja'far Aḥmad ibn Sa'īd
*(d. 1163) (Central Andalusia)*

# THE GARDEN

The garden of green hillocks
dresses up for visitors
in the most beautiful colors


as if a young woman's dowry
were spread out
glittering with gold necklaces


or as if someone had poured out
censers of musk powder
mixed with the purest aromatic oils.


Birds trill on the branches
like singing girls
bending over their lutes


and water falls continuously
like neckchains
of silver and pearls.

These are splendors of such perfection
they call to mind
the beauty of absolute certainty,
the radiance of faith.

'Abd Allāh ibn al-Simāk
*(d. 1145) (Granada)*

# THE BELOVED

Whoever looks into her eyes
is captured
as wine drinks the reason
of those that drink it.


Everyone fears her glance
except her.
Does the sword tremble
before the heart it pierces?


Weeping, I lifted my eyes
to her face;
the clouds were dispersed
by the sun of her forehead.


Remembering her waist
I tremble with love
like the doves
crying on the branches.

Her absence has left
black sadness in my chest
like the darkness that comes
when the sun goes.

'Umar ibn 'Umar
*(d. 1207) (Qāḍī of Córdoba and Sevilla)*

# DAYBREAK

When I saw Dawn come
shaking dew from her clear brow
I said to my love:

"I'm afraid the sun will discover
our secret;" but she said,

"Please God that my brother
not discover me!"

Sahl ibn Malik
*(1163-1249) (Granada)*

# MY BEAUTIFUL ONE

How beautiful she is!
And imagine that beauty
is only one of her qualities.
There is nothing more bewitching
than her movements.


She is more enchanting than the moon.
If you asked the real moon,
"What would you like to be?"
it is certain to reply,
"One of her halos."


When she looks at the real moon
it's as if she were looking
at her own face in a mirror.


The beauty spot on the page
of her cheek
punctuates the *nūns* written there
by the curls of her hair.

Once I went out with her when the
shelter of night and her cape
let me mingle the fire of my breath
with the fire of her flaming cheeks.

I clasped her as a miser clasps
his treasure, and bound her tightly
with the cords of my arms
lest she escape like a gazelle.

But my chastity did not permit me
to kiss her mouth
and my heart remained huddled
over its embers.

You may well marvel at one
who feels his entrails on fire
yet complains of thirst
while holding the quenching water
in his throat.

Ṣafwān ibn Idrīs
*(1165-1202) (Murcia)*

---

*nūn* — 25th letter of the Arabic alphabet (  ن  ).

# THE BATTLE

Oh God! The knights' banners
flutter like birds
encircling your enemies.

Lances punctuate the writing
of the swords;
dust like fine sand dries the ink;
blood perfumes it.

Ibn Sa'īd al-Maghribī
*(1214-1274) (Central Andalusia)*

# BLACK HORSE WITH WHITE CHEST

Black hindquarters, white chest:
he flies on the wings of the wind.


When you look at him you see dark night
opening, giving way to dawn.


Sons of Shem and Ham live harmoniously
in him, and take no care for the words
of would-be troublemakers.


Men's eyes light up when they see
reflected in his beauty


the clear strong black and white
of the eyes of beautiful women.

Ibn Sa'īd al-Maghribī

# THE WIND

There is no better procuress
than the wind
because it lifts garments
and uncovers hidden
parts of the body

weakens the resistance
of branches
and makes them lean over
and kiss the faces of pools.

No wonder the wind is used
as a go-between
to carry messages back and forth
between friends and lovers.

Ibn Sa'īd al-Maghribī

# THE FOUNTAIN

What a beautiful fountain
bombarding the sky with shooting stars
that leap agile as acrobats.


Gushing loops of water slide out
and race toward the basin
like terrified vipers.


Used to running furtively
underground, the water flees
when it enters an open space.


Resting peacefully in its new place
the bubbling water smiles
revealing pretty teeth,


a mouth so sweet
enamored trees bend over and kiss it.

Ibn al-Rā'i'ah
*(13th century) (Sevilla)*

71

# WHITE STALLION WITH BLACK MARKINGS ON HIS HOOVES

Can that be a horse
passing in front of my eyes
or a shooting star
swift as a lightning bolt
set off by a storm?

Dawn lent him her first rays
as a veil and raced
along with him in admiration.

Now he flees when Dawn comes
to reclaim her veil
and she cannot catch him.

When he charges the enemy
stars grow too tired to follow
and clouds lose track of him.

Oh, what a prodigy!
But if he belongs to the order of
planets, how did he get
dust on his feet?

Look at him.
No wonder he is massive.
His coat is of molten gold.


Musk powder has outlined in black
each of his four hooves.

Ibn Abī l-Ḥaytham
*(d. 1232) (Sevilla)*

# THE SUN

Look at the beautiful sun:
as it rises, it shows one golden eyebrow,
plays miser with the other one,

but we know that soon
it will spread out a radiant veil
over all.

A marvelous mirror
that appears in the East
only to hide again at dusk.

The sky is saddened
when the sun leaves
and puts on mourning robes.

I believe that falling stars
are nothing more
than sky's gem-hard tears.

Ibn Abī l-Ḥaytham

# FESTIVAL BY THE RIVER

Oh, look at the boats
plunging into the race
like chargers
one after the other.


Earlier the neck
of the river was bare;
now in the darkness
it is full of jewels.


The lights are stars,
their reflections, lances
stabbing the breast
of the river.


Like timid rabbits
escaping the falcon
the little boats flee
on their oar-feet

from the sloops
swooping down
on the wings
of their sails.

Ibn Lubbāl
*(d. 1187) (Jérez)*

# GIFT OF A MIRROR

I send you this marvelous mirror:
let your face rise
over its far horizon
like a moon of good fortune.


Then you will have to admit
how beautiful you are
and will forgive me
the passion I feel for you.


And though your image is elusive,
it is still more accessible,
more benevolent,
and a better keeper of promises
than you are!

Ibn al-Ṣābūnī
*(13th century) (Sevilla)*

# TO A PERSIAN REED BLOWN ABOUT BY THE WIND

Look at the reed
rocked by the wind
bending over our wine cups.

Was the dew she drank
not enough,
and she must now
wave her plumes about
in search of wine?

The way she moves
her slender waist
pleases the eyes
and the soul.

Let's give her a drink
from our glasses.
Since she is tipsy,
we can forgive her
for kissing us on the head.

Abū l-Ḥajjāj ibn 'Utba
*(13th century) (Sevilla)*

# THE DANCER

His manifold movements
toy with hearts.
He removes his garments
and is clothed in enchantment.


Supple as a branch
playful as a gazelle
his undulating motions
dally with the intelligence
of onlookers
as fate makes playthings of men.


And when he presses down on his head
with his feet
he is like a well-tempered sword
bent double
tip touching the pommel.

Ibn Kharūf
*(d. 1205) (Córdoba)*

Al-Mu'tamid, the "Poet-King" of Sevilla, reigned from 1068 to 1091. He was dethroned and then exiled to Aghmāt (Morocco) by the Berber Almoravids whom he himself had invited to Spain to help the Moorish rulers fight Alfonso VI. He died in captivity in Aghmāt in 1095. With his exile the great age of Islamic culture began to decline in Spain. The Almoravids, although they became quite "Hispanisized" over the years, did not even speak Arabic well, and thus had little feeling for the classical Arabic culture. Their courts could not provide the hospitable surroundings and support for poetry that Al-Mu'tamid had provided, though his love for poetry is probably unique among rulers of any age.

# REMEMBERING SILVES

Well, Abū Bakr,
greet my home place in Silves
and ask the people there
if, as I think, they still remember me.


Greet the Palace of the Balconies
on behalf of a young man
still nostalgic for that place.


Warriors like lions lived there
and white gazelles
in what beautiful forests
and in what beautiful lairs!


How many pleasurable nights I spent
in the shadow of the palace
with women of opulent hips
and delicate waists:


blonds and brunettes.
My soul remembers them
as shining swords and dark lances.

With one girl I spent
many delicious nights
beside the bend of the river.
Her bracelet resembled
the curve of the current


and as the hours went by
she offered me the wine
of her glance or that of her glass
and sometimes that of her lips.


The strings of her lute
wounded by the plectrum
caused me to shiver
as if I had heard a melody
played by swords on the
neck tendons of the enemy.

When she took off her cloak
and revealed her waist,
a flowering willow branch,
it was like a bud
opening to reveal the flower.

King Al-Mu'tamid of Sevilla
*(Reigned 1068-1091)*

# NIGHT OF FESTIVITIES

To tell the truth
I drank wine that spread out
a radiance of its own

from the time night started
to unfold its dark cloak

until the full moon rose in Gemini
like a king at the apex
of magnificence and splendor.

Bright stars surged out
vying with each other
to come close to the moon
and add their brilliance to hers.

Later when the moon
wanted to go westward
she raised Orion above her head
as a canopy

and the stars followed her
like flanking battalions
with the Pleiades as their banner.


So it is with me here on earth.
I walk amid squadrons of beautiful women
who add luster to high rank.


And though the weapons of my warriors
scatter darkness
the wine handed round by young women
fills us with light


and though the slave girls keep singing
and playing on their zithers,
my knights keep drumming out tunes
with their swords on enemy helmets.

King Al-Mu'tamid of Sevilla

## AL-MU'TAMID AND HIS FAMILY
## GO INTO EXILE

I will forget everything
except that morning
beside the Guadalquivir
when they were taken onto the ships
like the dead to their graves.


Jostling crowds lined both banks
to see them, precious pearls,
adrift on the foam of the river.


Young girls dropped their veils,
clawed their faces
and ripped their clothes.


The moment they left,
an endless commotion let loose
a clamorous outcry
of farewells and laments.

The departing ships were driven
along by sobs
as a lazy caravan is urged on
by the camel driver's song.


How many tears poured into the water!
How many broken hearts were borne away!

Ibn al-Labbānah
*(d. 1113) (Denia)*

# THE PRISONER IN AGHMĀT SPEAKS TO HIS CHAINS

I say to my chains,
don't you understand?
I have surrendered to you.
Why, then, have you no pity,
no tenderness?


You drank my blood.
You ate my flesh.
Don't crush my bones.


My son Abu Hasim sees me
fettered by you and turns away
his heart made sore.


Have pity on an innocent boy
who never knew fear
and must now come begging to you.


Have pity on his sisters
innocent like him
who have had to swallow poison
and eat bitter fruit.

Some of them are old enough
to understand and I fear
they will go blind from weeping.

The others are now too young
to take it in and open their mouths
only to nurse.

King Al-Mu'tamid of Sevilla